CONFRONTING
EVIL

ALSO BY BUD HARRIS, PHD

Sacred Selfishness: A Guide to Living a Life of Substance

Aging Strong: The Extraordinary Gift of a Longer Life

The Journey into Wholeness: A Jungian Guide to Discovering the Meaning of Your Life's Path

Becoming Whole: A Jungian Guide to Individuation

The Midnight Hour: A Jungian Perspective on America's Current Pivotal Moment

Students Under Siege: The Real Reasons Behind America's Ongoing Mass Shootings and How to Stop Them

Radical Hope and the Healing Power of Illness: A Jungian Guide to Exploring the Body, Mind, Spirit Connection to Healing

The Search for Self and the Search for God: Three Jungian Lectures and Seminars to Guide the Way

Cracking Open: A Memoir of Struggling, Passages, and Transformation

The Father Quest: Rediscovering an Elemental Force

Resurrecting the Unicorn: Masculinity in the 21st Century

The Fire and the Rose: The Wedding of Spirituality and Sexuality

CO-AUTHORED WITH MASSIMILLA HARRIS, PHD

Into the Heart of the Feminine: Facing the Death Mother Archetype to Reclaim Love, Strength, and Vitality

Like Gold Through Fire: Understanding the Transforming Power of Suffering

The Art of Love: The Craft of Relationships: A Practical Guide for Creating the Loving Relationships We Want

CONFRONTING EVIL

A Jungian Guide to Searching for
Light in the Heart of Darkness

BUD HARRIS, PHD

Daphne
Publications

Confronting evil: a jungian guide to searching for light in the heart of darkness by Bud Harris.

DAPHNE PUBLICATIONS, AN IMPRINT OF SPES, INC.

Harris, Clifton T. Bud
Confronting evil: a jungian guide to searching for light in the heart of darkness / Bud Harris.

ISBN: 978-0-578-81782-8 Nonfiction
1. Jungian psychology 2. Personal growth

Library of Congress Control Number: 2016908974
Spes, Inc., Asheville, NC

Cover and Interior Design: Courtney Tiberio

CONTENTS

"The force which threatens to blow the world asunder resides not in the clouds or mountains but in the invisible heart of the atom. The inner force, too, which, like the power of the atom, can either remake or shatter civilization resides in the smallest unit of society, the individual. The individual is the secret advance base from which the power sets out to invade committee rooms, mothers' meetings, county councils, parliaments, continents and nations."

—Laurens van der Post

FOREWORD

The very existence of evil and its mysterious and dramatic nature has presented us with one of the most difficult issues we have to face as human beings, personally and socially. For years we have lived in an age that is anxiouly focused on security and the good life, while overlooking or trivializing the formidable powers of evil growing in our culture.

As I began my reflections on developing this material for a lecture I presented in 2014, I had some difficulty defining evil. Finally, I settled on my own definition of it. I consider anything that causes a wound to the soul of a human being as evil. This wound may be to the soul personally or collectively. Experts in Post Traumatic Stress Disorders now tell us that war creates wounds to the souls of people fighting and involved in them. But many other events besides wars create wounds to our souls. Violence, abuse, betrayal, serious illnesses, the loss of loved ones, natural disasters and many other things you can probably name fall into this category. Soul wounds impair our ability to trust in life, often in ourselves, and in our capacity to love and be loved.

It is very hard for me, and I think for most of us, to think about evil and to try and understand it in profound yet non-intellectual ways. Most of us prefer to deny it, distance ourselves from it, and intellectualize ourselves from it. We often prefer to create a bubble of innocence around ourselves which is self-imposed naiveté. We have a hard time accepting its reality. Yet we are also at least dimly aware that the effect of ignoring the evils all around us is also a way of being engaged in them. If our denial fails we may become stuck in shock and dismay or, in some cases, begin to blame ourselves or even to identify with its perpetrators. I have seen these responses often enough in victims of abuse. In addition, we have a hard time seeing how we are participating in inflicting soul wounds through our attitudes and social and institutional structures while we are simply living our daily lives. But we also fear looking into our personal and collective shadows, the dark unconscious parts of ourselves, because we are afraid we might find evil there. Certainly Dr. Freud tended to think in that direction, and so do some of our more fundamentalist Christian groups. But Dr. Jung didn't think that way and neither do I. Yet, people can use their shadow characteristics to do evil things.

Today, evil confronts us on many levels, in our private lives and in society. Creating a future that values life and human beings depends on finding the courage today to face and confront evil and seek to understand it. We are challenged to find a way to overcome evil without creating another form of evil in its place. A task neither simple nor easy.

In this book I share some of my thoughts about evil—when it can be transformed, when it can be prevented, and how we should consider confronting it when neither of these possibilities are present. We will also think about what the different meanings of evil might be in our landscape of life in general, and in Jungian individuation process in specific. This journey looks deeply into the human and psychological dimensions of evil and how the shadow sides of our personality are intertwined with it. During this journey we look at evil from a personal, an archetypal, and a collective perspective.

Let me also remind you that when we begin to study subjects like evil a lot of emotion and history can be stirred up. So, I ask you to remember that I am sharing a point of view that I hope will stimulate and challenge you—but I am not trying to convince you of anything. In addition, please be careful and pay attention to your own responses because when we are discussing evil, it can invade us and affect our shadows and vulnerabilities before we know it.

While I was developing this lecture and this book, I had to remember Jung's warning (CW, Vol. 10) that, "The sight of evil kindles evil in the soul—there is no getting away from this fact. The victim is not the only sufferer; everybody in the vicinity of the crime, including the murderer, suffers with him (or her.)" And yet, I found my work through this material a kind of a breakthrough to a new level of consciousness and a new level of appreciation for the capacities of the human heart.

At the end of each section, you will have the opportunity that I give in workshops to go deep within and reflect upon questions that may stir strong feelings inside you...Use them as guideposts to listen to yourself.

I would like to invite you to journal your thoughts and your feelings—to write, to draw, to even scribble...and take your time. This is important work. Feel free to change your mind, to add more at a later time, and to expand to a larger personal journal. Be creative and take risks. Look deep within as you meet and discover your authentic self.

Remember, you are not trying to "fix" yourself or anyone else. You are learning how to treasure who you really are...and your life. Even though this journey may begin with the shock of confronting the effects of evil, it is also allowing you to go deeper, perhaps more than you have ever imagined, in an effort to understand yourself and the life around you.

PART ONE

The Nature of Evil

"Knowing your own darkness is the best method for dealing with the darknesses of other people. One does not become enlightened by imagining figures of light, but by making the darkness conscious. The most terrifying thing is to accept oneself completely. Your visions will become clear only when you can look into your own heart. Who looks outside, dreams; who looks inside, awakes."

—Carl Jung

DISCOVERING EVIL

Not long ago a friend of mine was jogging through a park in Atlanta. Suddenly, he came upon a body lying on the jogging path. My friend recognized the person lying there as a fellow jogger that he had known for years. It turned out that his fellow jogger had been robbed and murdered shortly before my friend discovered him. My friend doesn't believe that he will ever get completely over that experience.

Because of how dramatically evil affects us when it is close to home I have found that it is a difficult and confusing topic to discuss. To begin with, most of us simply don't want to look at it directly. In general, we want to deny it and have it be somewhere else, like in the Middle East, Africa, or the inner city. We don't deny that terrible things have happened and are happening. But we continue to delude ourselves by saying that it is somebody else, somewhere else, who is doing them.

In the years in which I worked in the inner city I began to realize that, almost without our knowing it, we have been so brainwashed by our rationalistic and materialistic ways of thinking that we have formed a frame of reference that leaves little space in our vision of life, or how we think life is or should be, for a principle of human destructiveness. And even when we see the evidence of this destructiveness all around us, as my friend did, we prefer not to believe that the evils we see exist in our lives and in the sphere of our spiritual development. We prefer to think, to rationalize, and to take a simplistic, pragmatic point of view that the evil around us could be eliminated by things such as more education, a better political system, a better economic system, or better psychological conditioning. We also seem to think that a commitment to one more war, whether it is actual or social, can solve our problems.

But what happens when we ask ourselves: if these things are the answer, why aren't we doing them? We don't have to follow this line of thinking very far until we must consider that evil really is a force in the world, and we need to accept that reality. But for most of us, accepting this reality challenges us to overhaul our whole worldview, and that can be a very painful and difficult task.

We are challenged to overhaul our worldview because we all tend to live our lives unconsciously. This means we live in a state referred to in the East as Maya, or a state of illusion. When we default to this very human approach to living, we are unconsciously trapped in our history, traditions, and the influences and values of our family's social groups and society; we have not been taught to seek understanding of these things in a profound way. Even if we know better than the way we are living, in many cases we will find it difficult to act on what we know. The reason is that if we act on this understanding we become committed to change, and therefore feel our identity, our relationships, and the way of life we rely on are in danger. Unless we are forced by the dark side of life's events, we rarely seek to understand the foundations of our worldview in order to become released from it.

I think it is interesting to note the great religions focus on awakening from this state of illusion. For example, when asked if he was enlightened the Buddha replied, "No, I am awake." The Sanskrit roots of the word *Buddha* mean "one who has awakened." The word is related to the Sanskrit words meaning "understanding" and "intelligence." A person who has awakened can therefore be said to be "one who knows"— one who has awakened to the true nature of reality. Two of Jesus' miracles address this same point metaphorically when he makes the blind see and the deaf hear. And a major purpose in Jungian analysis is to bring healing, wholeness, and meaning into our lives by discovering the truth— being able to see the truth—of our own reality.

Dr. Jung clearly emphasized that without the intervention of consciousness—the result of seeking a deeper understanding of our experiences, ourselves, and our personal and collective reality—our end will be as dark as our beginning. In fact, the more we refuse to seek consciousness the more we will be inviting the events that will challenge our worldview.

He goes further, quoting the Codex Bezae apocryphal insertion at Luke 6:4 to emphasize this point (CW, Vol. 11, par. 743): "Man, if indeed thou knowest what thou doest, thou art blessed: but if thou knowest not, thou art cursed, and a transgressor of the law." Dr. Jung continues in another place, "Before the bar of nature and fate, unconsciousness is never accepted as an excuse; on the contrary, there are severe penalties for it."

Please keep in mind that it is in this spirit to help us know and understand ourselves better that I am offering this book.

It usually takes a shock of some kind to force us to begin overhauling our world view.

This is true because it means we have to begin confronting our own shadow sides. It may also mean that we have to cultivate and refine our powerful emotions. Pragmatists tend to want to ignore their emotions out of fear the emotions will lead them astray—which, in fact, repressed crude and uncultivated emotions certainly can. But, without our emotions we are not engaged in life. We have numbed ourselves out; we have buried our passions and have trouble rousing ourselves out of passivity into action. Then when we finally act, the things we do seem either too little, too late, or too harsh to be effective. We see examples of these tendencies in couples and families all too frequently. Most of the time we find it easier to live in denial, or even if we accept the force of evil as a reality, we project it far away from ourselves. It is a much more challenging task to accept Jung's advice to begin looking into our own shadows, looking at the demons and devils within ourselves as the foundation or starting point for looking at evil in general. This necessary inner journey enables us to face the complexity of evil—its paradoxes and mysteries, its archetypal force—so that we can clearly see and handle its presence in our lives rather than unconsciously enabling it.

Thoughts and Questions to Ponder...

As you finish reading and reflecting upon this first intense section, find a quiet, comfortable, safe place and take a few moments to settle into yourself.

Take some deep breaths and let your mind wander back over what you have read. Now let me invite you to spend some time writing on the pages we have provided or in your journal about what you have experienced while you were reading. What were some of the ideas and feelings that came up in you?

As you continue you might consider these questions:

What are some of the ways you were conditioned while growing up to deny evil and have it be somewhere else?

As you grew up, how did your family, friends, culture, religion, and education teach you to think about the nature of human destructiveness?

How does accepting the reality of evil as a force in the world challenge the worldview you actually live by?

Ask yourself how you have seen the reality of this quotation from Dr. Jung show up in your life: "Before the bar of nature and fate, unconsciousness is never accepted as an excuse; on the contrary, there are severe penalties for it."

Other Thoughts...

HOW EVIL IS BORN

If we really want to listen to Jung or to any of our great religious traditions, and want to see the force of evil in the world realistically (or for that matter, to be able to see into ourselves and truly understand how we are living,) we must break out of our rationalistic, materialistic way of thinking. After all, Jung is clear (Modern Man in Search of a Soul, p. 212) that the gods we are called to overthrow are the idolized values of our conscious world. So, then the first thing we must do is to open ourselves up to being able to look at life and into ourselves poetically, mythologically, and symbolically. Jung says (CW 18, par 627 and 630) that, "Now we have no symbolic life, and we are all badly in need of the symbolic life. Only the symbolic life can express the needs of the soul—the daily needs of the soul, mind you." Now listen carefully, these are powerful statements. Jung continues by saying the symbolic life is the foundation of a life of depth and meaning. Without a symbolic foundation we are in danger of pursuing make-believe lives based on the cultural ideas of "the good life" or other people's definitions of how we should live.

We are in danger of becoming alienated from our gifts and from our life's purpose. When our personal and collective lives are hollow in this sense, the door to evil is opened on many levels.

When we think about the symbolic life, we are reminded of stories in mythology, whether in actual myths or in the stories of our great religions. Our timeless myths and religious stories are metaphors to give shape to, and enable us to understand, the universal, archetypal realities which underlie our psychic experiences, our profound experiences of being human. These are also the underlying forces that can unconsciously drive our lives and compel our behaviors. Having some knowledge of this way of perceiving life is an essential requirement if we (in my professional language that means our egos) are going to be able to have a knowledge of, and a relationship with, the deeper layers of our psyche and the reality of who we really are. When our ego—the part of the psyche that we think of as "I", our conscious mind, our everyday brain that tries to run our daily lives—lacks these ways of understanding ourselves and life, we are cut off from being able to relate to our Self, with a capital "S", our own center, the ground of our own being. Jung defined the Self as a greater entity, which includes the ego and also incorporates the personal and collective unconscious. Our dreams, our great emotions, our potentials, and our life force come from the Self. The archetypes of the collective unconscious dwell in the Self as well. Understanding our interior lives depends upon our ability to think and feel symbolically, as does our ability to have a more grounded perspective on life and a sense of inner meaning and security. In other words, for us to feel that our life has a purpose and a unique value in the scheme of things, we must be able to think and live symbolically. And, without this ability and the inner-relatedness within our interior lives, our ability to live without fear and to have peace of mind will be very limited.

Without this inner understanding our lives will be confined to shallow levels of meaning—dry, cold, or overly sentimental ways of engaging life emotionally, a limited capacity to give and receive love. And equally significant, it will be easy for the unconscious pressures within us and in our complexes to take us over, forcing us to live them out without our realizing what is really motivating our actions.

Thoughts and Questions to Ponder...

As you finish reading the section, reflect on the theme that your knowledge, not your understanding (for knowledge comes from both the heart and the mind,) of your inner self grounds you in your purpose in life and makes it possible to become responsible citizens.

In this process of seeking to know yourself, how does Dr. Jung's admonition that "...the gods we are called to overthrow are the idolized values of our conscious world" affect you? Are you aware that you have idolized values? How do you think they may structure your life?

Pause and sit back. Then relax and take a breath. Ask yourself how some of the ways in which you define the "good life" have structured the way you live. And, ask yourself if how you define the good life can alienate you from your gifts and the purpose of your life. Does the quotation above resonate with you?

When you think of the symbolic life spend a few minutes considering fairy tales, myths, and religious stories. Think of these tales about eating the poisonous apple, being swallowed by a whale, or being abandoned to die in a dark forest. Or remember Hansel and Gretel being seduced by the evil witch's beautiful home made of cake and candy that lured them into the illusion of sweetness and safety. Ask yourself the question, "Isn't it the symbolic approach to life that challenges us to see it clearly and, in the face of it, live life to the fullest?"

Write your answers on these pages or in your journal.

Other Thoughts...

EVIL AS AN ARCHETYPE

Many of us are aware that humanism, at times, sees good and evil in relative terms depending on one's perceptions. Because this perspective often coincides with how we work with our shadows, Jung's work has frequently been confused with that humanistic point of view. However, Jung was very clear that he saw evil as real, and thought we must recognize it as real. Lucifer, Satan, and the Devil are archetypal images. They have different archetypal insinuations, and they represent different faces of how the archetype of evil can channel our destructive energies.

For us to be able to understand the reality of ourselves and of evil as well, it is helpful to know a little bit about archetypes and archetypal images. In describing the nature of archetypes, Jung says (CW, Vol. 10, par 395), "An archetype is like an old water-course along which the water of life has flowed for centuries digging a deep channel for itself." Therefore, it has become a pattern in our psyche that directs the flow of a particular portion of our life energy. We can "see" this energy through our emotional responses to it, and then through the images and ideas that evolve from our experiences of it. For example, in the Judeo-Christian heritage, we see the destructive force or forces in life imaged in the ideas of Satan, Lucifer, the Devil, and so on. The destructive force in the world was a reality for Jung, which also meant it was an archetypal force inherent in our nature. The image it takes depends upon how we respond to it and how we have been taught to respond to it. The Devil is an archetypal image, but it doesn't fully define the archetype, which has many different images and experiences in different cultures and religions.

Jung's disagreement with the Catholic Church was that during his lifetime the church considered evil as an absence of good and not a reality in itself. Jung understood that we have a great reluctance to confront the many dimensions of evil itself, both in life and in ourselves. But he also thought that in general, nothing could be transformed or fully dealt with unless it was first acknowledged as a reality. And that we cannot learn how to deal with the complexities of evil until we can acknowledge and confront it as a reality.

Thoughts and Questions to Ponder...

As you relax and think about this brief section, what are some of your thoughts and reflections around the idea that evil is a force in reality and not just an absence of good?

Would you agree that in order to deal with the complexities of evil we must first acknowledge and confront it as a reality?

Have you seen ways in which you, your ego, have denied the existence of evil? Did certain events force you to acknowledge its existence? If so, can you write a short story or fairy tale of your own about these events?

Other Thoughts...

PART TWO

Personal Evil

"If I admit with Richard Wright in that poem 'Between the World and Me' that evil goes into me as does the good, then I'm obliged to study myself and make a choice. For I must know that the battles I wage are within myself. The wars I fight are in my mind. They are struggles to prevent the negative from overtaking the positive, and to prevent the good from eradicating all the negative and rendering me into an apathetic, useless organism, which has no struggle, no dynamic, and no life."

—Maya Angelou

THE SHADOW AND THE SELF

When talking about evil from the Jungian perspective I believe we should begin in that archetypal area of our personal unconscious that we refer to as the shadow. In general, our shadow is all of the parts of ourselves, potentially bad and good, that we denied growing up. We usually repress them in our efforts to form a personality that would be acceptable and give us as much safety as possible in our early circumstances. We often look to our dreams to shed some light in this area of ourselves and what is going on in it. The situation becomes more challenging when our unconscious is telling us through our dreams that we need to look into our shadows.

A good example is Marie. In her mid-forties, she initially came to see me because she was having a recurring dream. In the dream she was being chased by women who were dressed as Nazis. They wore the brown shirts with the red armbands with swastikas on them. In her dream, these ferocious, determined women were coming closer and closer to Marie as she cowered in terror in a closet in the basement of her home. Marie saw them as driven, machine-like creatures who totally disregarded human and feminine values.

The terror Marie felt is typical of our response to evil when it threatens. In the dream, the female figures represent the shadow side of Marie's personality, as same-sex dream figures do in Jungian psychology. The shadow, as I have said, represents the dark, feared, unwanted side of our personality. It contains the cut-off, repressed qualities in our personalities that we rejected in order to become the person we wanted to be, or needed to be, so we could feel safe and accepted as we grew up. These qualities now feel "evil" to Marie because to recognize them and accept them would threaten the security of her self-image. But the Self, the voice of greater intelligence within her, is showing Marie that these elements in her personality are becoming threatening. In some ways, they also picture what she is doing to herself. And she must, in this case, find a way to recognize and integrate them or live with an increasing sense of unhappiness.

On this plane in our psyche, we are dealing with a fairly simple level of evil that, when recognized and integrated, can be transformed to strengthen and broaden who we are.

As Marie worked with these images by reflecting upon her history, making associations to the images, and doing active imagination with them, she discovered they represented her ability to achieve worth through attaining desired goals and developing a feeling of control over her life and future. In other words, they were symbolizing her denied sense of personal power. This sounds good so far...

But then Marie realized that by failing to recognize her worth and power, her inner need to do this had taken on a devastating negative capacity that had pursued her relentlessly with self-criticism and self-doubt. She was treating herself like an object, without love, respect, and dignity. She also recognized that she was following in her mother's and grandmother's footsteps because she was beginning to create a negative atmosphere around herself that echoed the feelings of misery and scarcity in their lives. She feared that if this negativity continued, she could end up dying of cancer in the same way her mother had.

There are several important things we can learn about evil from this simple example. The first one is that to acknowledge the power in these negative images doesn't mean to embrace them. It means to recognize them and to begin to search for the meaning behind them. This is the only way we can discover if the intelligence of the Self is directing a part of our individuation process through these dream images.

The next thing we can learn is that some kinds of evil, some kinds of negative archetypal energy can be healed and transformed through self-knowledge and integration.

The third thing for us to consider is that what we think of as evil can rarely be transformed through direct confrontation. In other words, to fight evil can frequently cause it to strengthen and arm itself in order to fight back harder. For instance, if Marie tried to directly confront what we might call her negative attitudes, she would most likely find them very resilient. Then, her self-criticism would escalate in the face of her struggles and difficulties in trying to overpower these negative aspects of herself that were making her miserable.

The fourth thing we might notice is that Marie felt terrified in the dream. Whenever we feel a major emotion like terror, rage, intense anger, or hurt, we are probably touching a significant archetypal issue in our lives that can go in a very destructive direction if we are not careful with it. Overall, I think that we can see that what initially appeared as evil in the dream is a call for

Marie to develop more consciousness in order to better fulfill her life and future.

The example of Marie's dream shows us that the shadow can have two aspects—one that is dangerous and the other that is valuable. As we also saw, whether Marie's shadow became a destructive force in her life or helped her build a new life depended upon the way she approached it through her dream material. However, deciding how to approach these images isn't always so simple, as Jung's associate Dr. Louise Marie von Franz points out in chapter three of Man and His Symbols. Dr. von Franz quotes a story from the Koran in order to illustrate the paradoxical nature of our shadows, of evil and the nature of the decisions we face on this journey. Dr. von Franz writes:

The ethical difficulties that arise when one meets one's shadow are well described in the 18th Book of the Koran. In this tale, Moses meets Khidr ('the Green One' or 'first angel of God') in the desert. They wander along together, and Khidr expresses his fear that Moses will not be able to witness his deeds without indignation. If Moses cannot bear with him and trust him, Khidr will have to leave.

Presently Khidr scuttles the fishing boat of some poor villagers. Then, before Moses' eyes he kills a handsome young man, and finally he restores the fallen wall of a city of unbelievers. Moses cannot help expressing his indignation, so Khidr has to leave him. Before his departure, however, he explains the reasons for his actions: By scuttling the boat he actually saved it for its owners because pirates were on their way to steal it. As it is, the fishermen can salvage it. The handsome young man was on his way to commit a crime, and by killing him Khidr saved his pious parents from infamy. By restoring the wall, two pious young men were saved from ruin because their treasure was buried under it. Moses, who had been so morally indignant, saw too late that his judgment had been too hasty. Khidr's doings had seemed to be totally evil, but in fact they were not.

Dr. von Franz continues by saying:

Looking at this story naively, one might assume that Khidr is the lawless, capricious, evil shadow of pious, law-abiding Moses. But this is not the case. Khidr is much more the personification of some secret creative actions of the Godhead.

...or, in my language, the creative intelligence of the Self.

We can see from these examples how, in them, the Jungian view of the shadow and evil—and how we work with them—is paradoxical, and how the participation of the intelligence of the Self forming our life, from within, complicates this entire picture.

Thoughts and Questions to Ponder...

While you were reading Marie's dream what kind of thoughts and feelings came up in you?

What were your reflections while reading that what initially appeared evil in Marie's dream turned out to be a call to develop more consciousness and to enlarge her personality?

Can you journal more of your thoughts about the idea that the shadow has two aspects—one dangerous and one valuable? Do you agree?

Why do you think you, or we, are afraid to confront and seek to know y/our shadow?

Have you had dreams of things that appeared evil that scared you? In remembering them do you now see them in a different way?

Other Thoughts...

THE PARADOX OF OBSTACLES

But there are also other situations that we need to consider. A few years ago, another woman, Janice, came in to see me with a recurring dream. In this dream, she was being chased through a pitch black movie theater, up one aisle and down another. She was being chased through a pitch black movie theater up one aisle and down another by a large man trying to kill her with a butcher knife. Janice told me that her previous therapist suggested that she simply stop, turn around, face the man and embrace him. Then Janice said, "I just couldn't do that. It was too scary."

Of course, she was right not to do that. We all need to listen to our fear before acting. Options like screaming for help or running out of an exit didn't seem open to her. My response was that the dream was telling her something else. I believe it was telling her that we needed to work very carefully on healing her past, healing her fear, and developing her ability to like, nourish, and take loving care of herself as a support to become more self-reliant and self-empowered. Within a few years, her whole life had changed. It is always interesting to see how fast our symptoms may recede once we have energetically committed to our inner work. Because Janice listened to her fear in her dreams and didn't naively seek a solution to it, what seemed at first to be devastating, evil and destructive, became a turning point in her life.

In a situation like Janice's, the 39th hexagram in the *I Ching*, "Obstacles" or "Obstructions" can give us a helpful perspective. In his translation, Richard Wilhelm says in this hexagram we are facing a dangerous abyss before us and a steep mountain behind us. We cannot retreat or advance. Our obstacles cannot be overcome directly. The advice from the *I Ching* is to join forces with friends of a like mind and put oneself under the leadership of someone equal to the situation and listen to them with both ears. R. L. Wing, in his translation of this same hexagram, suggests that, like flowing water meeting an obstacle, we must pause and increase in strength and volume until we flow over the obstacle. This is what Janice was doing in her work with me. She was pausing, and through working with her unconscious, building up the inner strength and substance to successfully overflow the obstacles in her life.

Thoughts and Questions to Ponder...

As you explore more about the ideas in this section in your journal, what can you say about our need to listen more closely to our fear about our shadows?

What is your response to the *I Ching*'s suggestion that when faced with an obstacle we may need to pause and build up the strength, as flowing water does, in order to flow over it? What could this advice mean in your life?

In what ways have you built up rigid structures in your past that are now obstacles that keep you from living fully, limiting your gifts and purpose in life? Are there some ways in which you might be doing that now?

With what you have read and reflected on so far why do you think so much of our entertainment is dominated by a sense of violence?

Other Thoughts...

THE TERRORIST WITHIN

Now let us look at another dream. Grady is a middle-aged professional man. By all appearances, he is fairly successful. But he is wondering why he has been feeling a loss of energy for over a year, a low grade sense of misery— and why he wakes up every day with a gnawing sense of dissatisfaction. As we will see shortly, it doesn't make any difference whether he is a doctor, a dentist, a lawyer, a banker, a corporate executive, or whatever. Grady's recurring dream was that he was in a small city in the desert, probably Iraq, he said. In the dream he was in the second story, the top floor, of a large house firing a machine gun. The town was being overrun by an army of terrorists. In the background, a group of Middle Eastern women were making the warlike noise we hear them make at times, in support of the terrorists. Grady knew that if he were caught, he would be tortured and killed.

As we discussed the dream, we quickly realized that a desert pictured the emotional landscape that Grady lived in. He lived and worked in a determined way in an atmosphere that was achievement-oriented, competitive, anxious and, in the negative sense, very patriarchal. There were no feminine values present in his work environment. But "What in the world are these terrorists picturing in me?" he asked, "Can part of me be this evil and brutal?"

Of course, his Self has picked terrorists for this dream imagery for a reason. We naturally connect terrorists with evil. But the Jungian approach is to always search for the meaning in our images, including the meaning in how to face absolute evil. So Grady and I began to talk about the terrorists.

Our discussion went something like this: Terrorists not only want to kill us, they are willing to kill themselves in the process. This attitude shows us a kind of aggression that the psychoanalyst Eric Fromm calls *malignant aggression* in his books on evil and human destructiveness (*The Anatomy of Human Destructiveness* and *The Heart of Man: Its Genius for Good and Evil*). Malignant aggression is the kind of aggression that is meant to control life by destroying it and destroying our spirit of life. Malignant aggression is purely power-oriented. Its source usually comes from an extreme sense of despair that is based on helplessness and alienation. Remember that word, alienation— we are going to come back to it.

Jung says that the spirit of evil is fear and the negation of life (CW, Vol. 5, par. 551). Because terrorists, like the ones in Grady's dream, are one of the extreme examples of malignant aggression along with rapists, murderers, assassins, and mass-murderers, I want to take a few minutes to explore the source of this kind of evil. And, as you reflect on these matters later, you may join me in wondering why these themes are so predominant in our field of entertainment.

If we consider for a moment the horror of a high school student shooting teachers and classmates, we need to ask ourselves what is the source of this evil, this malignant aggression? Is it mental illness? Is it the presence of guns and a culture of violence? Or, are these types of things uniting with a deeper symptomatology in our society? Is there a kind of despair that surfaces through our most vulnerable young people, a despair of hopelessness, an inability to find a place in the tribe, or, in other words, alienation? Are we forcing our children into lives of feeling externally judged—being members of ability groups, teams, levels of performance, and organizations—on a collective scale to the point it is destroying their personal spirit of life?

And I think we must also ask ourselves how

much the way we have structured our schools reflects the structures that you and I are living by.

Later, as we were discussing his dream, Grady said, "Damn! Maybe I've created this inner desert. Maybe I have been so focused on my goals, wanting the best for myself and my family that I am actively negating some of the life around me, my life. Can the goals I thought were so good—the good intentions I've focused my life on, my ideals—actually be fostering these inner terrorists?" Now Grady is beginning to ask himself the right questions. He has to find the courage to face his life realistically, to step out of the cultural brainwashing of his history and listen to his inner life, beginning with the feelings he has denied.

Thoughts and Questions to Ponder...

While you were reading Grady's dream and our discussion of it did anything resonate with you?

Dr. Eric Fromm's idea that malignant aggression is power-oriented is a very important concept. Can you journal more about how this concept affected you? What more do you think and feel about it?

As you reflect upon Dr. Jung's statement that the spirit of evil is fear and the negation of life, what feelings are coming up in you? Are you surprised in any way?

Other Thoughts...

PART THREE

Collective Evil

"In my long experience of violence and meaninglessness in the modern world, of tension in modern societies, and of all the disorder accumulating and growing within societies and between cultures, never in the history of humankind has the world been so totally involved in a state of crisis as it is today. This statement does not apply only to the Western world, but also to the great civilizations of the Far East. It applies to all countries, primitive as well as sophisticated, democratic as well as totalitarian. We are all confronted with a strange kind of disorder and sense of meaninglessness that afflicts us."

—Laurens van der Post

LOSING THE COLLECTIVE MYTH

At this point, we might ask ourselves what creates these inner terrorists and are inner and outer terrorists created in similar ways? Eric Fromm is correct in concluding that despair and alienation create people who seek power and control, and the desire to transcend their situation by violence, even to themselves. But we also have to ask ourselves what happens when entire groups of people become disillusioned, humiliated and impoverished—when groups feel helpless and hopeless—when the structures of ideals and values that gave purpose and meaning to their lives have collapsed, failed them, or have been taken away from them? And when they may also feel worthless and victimized? In Jungian terms, we would say this group of people has lost the myth that supported their lives. These losses open the door for the archetype of evil to become the foundation of a new myth that brings meaning to them through power and destructiveness. We see examples of this condition in post-World War I Germany, in the Middle East today, and in segments of our own society.

It is also interesting to look at how we can

alienate and disenfranchise parts of ourselves until they become desperate actors in our unconscious and in our bodies. As Grady continued reflecting on his dream about the terrorists, he realized that he had focused so intently on his goals and certain values that he had become, in essence, a fundamentalist in how he lived his life. He was structuring himself in a way that disenfranchised and threatened to annihilate parts of himself – his emotional, feminine and feeling parts. He had lost his sense of knowing how to value his experiences and the way he was living. And he was beginning to realize that such a loss caused him to be unable to value himself as well. He also began to realize that his Self was sending him a message by showing that these disowned parts of himself have the power to strike back with force and poignancy. We also concluded that this dream was a gift of warning to him because these forces could escalate their attack into a stroke, a heart attack, a cancer, or some other serious form.

The point of this discussion about malignant aggression is that whether it is individual, societal, or personal, it is a call for consciousness—a call for a rock solid look at our reality and the courage to see how we hide from life and sabotage ourselves.

As Grady began to have an active imagination —to dialogue with the leader of the terrorists in his dream—he made some startling discoveries. The leader told him that, "We in the Middle East are passionate people. We are driven by feelings. Can't you see that we are the passion, the rage, and the love that can connect you to the essentials of life? Can't you see we are pictured as enemies because we are enemies to your arrogant, one-sided, over-controlled approach to life?" As he listened to this image in his shadow, Grady was beginning to get a sense for his need of the second kind of aggression that Eric Fromm wrote about. Fromm called this kind of aggression *benign aggression*. In this kind of aggression, our strength is directed towards preserving life and having a spirit of aggression and adventure in the support of life. If Grady can open his attitudes to preserving and fostering his inner life, his strength and energy will increase. So will his capacity to be more loving and more fully alive. He will be able to loosen his passions in how he lives, take more risks, quit dreading failure, and break his internalized cultural traditions. The capacity for benign aggression is a must to protect our love of life, our tender places, and our ability to be creative.

When Jung (CW Vol. 5, par. 531) wrote that

the spirit of evil is fear and negation, he went on to say that it infuses us with the poison of weakness and regression. He points out that for us to grow and transform fear must become a challenge and a task, because only boldness can deliver us from fear. He continues by saying that if the risks are not taken to grow, then the meaning of life is somehow violated and the future is condemned to hopeless staleness. As Grady has pondered his dream, he has gradually experienced his own sense of courage shifting from his former ideals of achievement and overcoming obstacles to preserving life, pursuing his inner journey and allowing his ambitions to reflect his love of life.

Thoughts and Questions to Ponder...

Now, let me ask you to sit back, relax, read the following quotation again, and journal your responses to it.

"But we also have to ask ourselves what happens when entire groups of people become disillusioned, humiliated and impoverished—when groups feel helpless and hopeless—when the structures of ideals and values that gave purpose and meaning to their lives have collapsed, failed them, or have been taken away from them? And when they may also feel worthless and victimized? In Jungian terms, we would say this group of people has lost the myth that supported their lives. These losses open the door for the archetype of evil to become the foundation of a new myth that brings meaning to them through power and destructiveness."

Where do you see the reality of these statements in the culture around you?

Here is another quotation to consider:

"It is also interesting to look at how we can alienate and disenfranchise parts of ourselves until they become desperate actors in our unconscious and in our bodies."

Let me invite you again to think about this statement and reflect and journal about how it might resonate with you.

Other Thoughts...

GAZING INTO THE FACE OF EVIL

Thinking about dreams of terrorists brings me to another point and that is, how do we respond when we have to look evil in the face? Jung makes a striking statement when he says that (CW, v. 9ii, Aion), "It is quite within the bounds of possibility for a man to recognize the relative evil of his nature, but it is a rare and shattering experience for him to gaze into the face of absolute evil." But this is exactly what we have to face when a person, group or society becomes possessed by the archetype of evil, or a myth dominated by this archetype. How can we face unrelenting malignant aggression? Well, I must admit that I don't really know the answer to this question. But there are two lines of thinking that inform me.

The first thing that I think is that we must do our best to take a clear moral stand against this kind of evil. This means that we must stand with strength and use the full force of benign aggression to preserve and protect life, even if it means we must become completely ruthless in our actions. And we must remember that to slip into denial, sentimental idealism, or to fight evil half-heartedly opens us to being contaminated and even absorbed by it. But we must stand not only with strength, but also with great humility, not righteousness. The nature of life teaches us repeatedly that we are unable to see the evil in the good, and the good that is in the evil, taking place in our lives.

In Goethe's great poetic drama *Faust*, we find Mephistopheles, the devil in the drama, complaining that people don't appreciate him because they don't realize that without him, nothing would ever happen in the world. When asked by Faust who he is, he replies that he is "part of that force which would do evil, yet forever works for the good." So, in the face of absolute evil, I think we must be able to respond with strength, and if necessary, ruthlessness, and yet with humility and a renewed search for consciousness.

There is another question we have to face as well. What happens when we are the victims of absolute evil? I have worked with people who have been tortured, abused as children and have been sex slaves. I can easily understand that these situations can be more than the human heart can stand. And yet, deep in our souls, there is the possibility of the resilience in the depth of our humanity that can heal and transcend these experiences. In order to illustrate this possibility, I would like to share a story with you that informs me. It is part of Sir Laurens van der Post's story which he relates in the film interview with him titled "Hasten Slowly." Sir Laurens, the author of over 20 books, was a great friend and biographer of Jung. As a British officer, he spent most of World War II in a Japanese prisoner of war camp for British soldiers, and from that experience he tells this story:

I remember a particularly nasty execution to which my friend Nicholas and I had to stand in formation with our young officers to watch. They were executing two soldiers who had gotten too close to the prison fence. The way these soldiers died was indescribably moving. One was tied between two posts driven into the ground and they had bayonet practice on him. The other was beheaded as he knelt on the ground. At the moment the execution started, a British officer standing between Nicholas and myself who was frail because he had been tortured, began to collapse. I said to myself this mustn't happen because it will spread.

I felt we must face this upright and look it in the eye, and I put my arm around this man, in a way the Japanese couldn't see, to hold him up. As I did, so I felt Nicholas from the other side instinctively doing the same thing. I felt the officer between us straighten up. We stood and looked at the man being bayoneted without flinching. I wanted to look away and pretend it wasn't happening, but a voice inside of me said you can't do that because you would be betraying the man who is being killed if you do that; you must go through it with him. That is your contribution here and now, you must go through it, you must be killed with him if you are going to understand what is going on.

This story has informed me as I live and work, for years. It helps me look reality, including suffering and evil, in the eye. It has helped me work with people who have suffered horrible things. And, it makes me thank God that I have never faced evil in this way—and it also makes me thank God for how in the face of such evil, the human spirit can respond with a depth of consciousness and humanity that can inspire and inform us all.

Thoughts and Questions to Ponder...

Please think some more about this quotation:

"Jung makes a striking statement when he says that (CW, v. 9ii, Aion), 'It is quite within the bounds of possibility for a man to recognize the relative evil of his nature, but it is a rare and shattering experience for him to gaze into the face of absolute evil.'"

Does this statement surprise you? What kinds of thoughts and feelings does it arouse in you?

What kind of range of emotions did Sir Laurens van der Post's story bring up as you read it?

Other Thoughts...

PART FOUR

Facing the Fire

"We do not know where we will be two, ten, or twenty years from now. What we can know, however, is that man suffers and that a sharing of suffering can make us move forward."

—Henri J. M. Nouwen

WHERE NEW LIFE BEGINS

Facing evil means facing the wounds to our souls. After World War Two, Sir Laurens van der Post, who was from South Africa, retreated into the wilds of Africa to heal himself and regain his sense of self. To continue this process of reconciliation with himself he wrote a book that ended up in the very moving film *Merry Christmas, Mr. Lawrence*, starring David Bowie, based on his experiences as a prisoner of war of the Japanese. We must grieve our soul wounds and seek inner reconciliation with ourselves. In many places in his writings, Dr. Jung pointed out that our wounds cannot be healed, nor our lives changed, until our wounds are fully accepted. This reality means we must accept the wounds to our souls that are caused by evil, and a major part of our acceptance relies on our capacity to grieve for our pain, for the innocence we have lost, and the depths of the effects on our humanity.

In the Old Testament portion of the Bible we find that the original words for evil and suffering are the same. It was in the language of the Greeks with its greater discrimination that the two words were separated. But, in our personal experiences they often remain intertwined as they did in my early history.

When I was a child my mother began a slow journey with cancer. Her journey ended when I was fourteen years old. That was when I learned that the price of love was grief. It was love's absence that finally taught me how much love matters. This was also a soul wound that at the time seemed evil. It was a long time before I could open my heart to love again, or to the grief and anger I had locked away in the same heart. I grew up in a culture that promoted desensitizing our hearts, in a nation that was turning away from love and admonishing us to hide everything beneath a positive attitude. I was taught to always say I was fine, period. And, don't let such things as sorrow slow down your work or ability to keep busy. I learned to live in the wasteland; I blindly followed, as if in a trance, the social norms for my age group and doing what other people valued and expected (as we often do when faced with soul wounds and the effects of evil.) Surprisingly, if you had asked me, I would have said that I was living my life authentically. Yet it was only later in my life after a crisis had forced me into a deep inner journey that I was able to excavate and face my old grief and mourn my loss. Then, stronger and wiser, I became free to love again.

Life generally finds a way to challenge us with a crisis when we have lapsed into taking our future, circumstances, and purpose for granted. I learned through hard struggles that whenever I face a crisis or trauma it is Dr. Jung's individuation process that moves me to face these events and become more engaged in life. Dr. Jung was strongly convinced that only a full engagement in life—through new confrontations with our reality, our history, our profound emotions, and, yes, our shadows—gives us the necessary material for the reflections that transform our personalities and how we are living our lives. Transformation mirrors the creative cycle of life; it is the cycle of life, death, and new birth. Life challenges us to participate in it as a continuing quest because it is a constant flow of these cycles. We experience the death aspect of these cycles very personally because they are often filled with conflict, betrayal, disappointment, and contentions with fate and evil. If we do not grieve what we are losing, what is dying and passing, these times can easily become ones of hopelessness and despair. And, I must say that accepting the full creative cycles is counter-cultural in this society which emphasizes instant gratification, getting back to normal, and the illusions of the "good life" at the expense of the challenges of growth and transformation.

Life has hit us between the eyes with this pandemic. A great deal that we love is being lost and threatened. Deaths are rising at an appalling rate. They are leaving too many of us facing painful, lonely deaths and many more families in shocked, isolated mourning with little support. Too many of our healthcare workers are facing days filled with loneliness, exhaustion, and grief. Our nation has lost its foundation of security in numerous ways, the foundation we relied on. Our present is filled with suffering, fear, and an uncertain path into the future.

Our current upheavals have also made us more aware of other levels of soul wounds in our country. Some of the strongest ones come from our history of systemic racial inequality. Others come from systemic income inequality, heartless physical and mental healthcare systems, and a broken justice system. Oh, so much! There is grief as a result of loving my country as well.

Our national and individual souls are wounded. Too many of us are brokenhearted and we aren't paying attention to our need to join together in our sorrow and mourn. If we cannot face the truth of our losses and our suffering, and find a healing way through them that brings us closer to completing our cycle of transformation, our fear and grief will continue to be increasingly sublimated into anger, aggression, and projecting blame onto other people and groups.

There is also another issue today. We are the daily victims of emotional and verbal abuse from demagogues, media groups, the internet, and supporting groups that are enchanted by power and cultivate fear in order to overshadow our capacity to love. They slam us daily with ongoing emotional violence. We can no more successfully tune them out than a child can find safety in his or her room while the parents are screaming and beating each other on the other side of the door. We must find a voice to speak out against this abuse, this kind of evil, and become able to grieve our pain while our wounds are raw and bleeding.

It may help us to remember our great religions put suffering at the top of their agendas because it is an inescapable fact of life. They follow this reality with compassion as a leading virtue. If we deny our own pain we will deny the pain of others and fail in our faith traditions and in the heart of our humanity. Survivors of our great crises have much to teach us about living through terrible times and conditions. The revered Holocaust survivor Elie Wiesel told us that the opposite of "love" is indifference. Indifference comes when we have buried our capacity to feel our pain. When we bury our grief we actually "bury it alive," and deep inside of us it devours our capacity to love. Another great teacher who survived the Nazi death camps, Viktor Frankl, teaches us that survival depends upon being oriented toward the future and toward a meaning to be fulfilled in the future. Dr. Martin Luther King, Jr., taught us that love must be strong, it must take risks and bind a community. Our great teachers and healers are clear that we must be willing to say what has been unsayable, face our pain and losses as a community, and remember when we mourn together the wounds to our souls will begin to heal.

As a young boy I learned that the price of love is grief. Since then I have learned that the well of love in our hearts is deeper than the well of grief. Being fully human means risking grief for love, and that both call for action. Grief demands action that brings compassion and healing love to ourselves and others. Love demands the kind of action that heals grief, opens our hearts, and fulfills our lives as members of the human family. We must speak up, mourn, grieve, and love while our painful journey is still going on. New life actually begins when we have found the courage to face and mourn for our losses and refuse to live in fear.

Thoughts and Questions to Ponder...

If you reflect on this quotation what kind of responses come up in you?

"Dr. Jung pointed out that our wounds cannot be healed, nor our lives changed, until our wounds are fully accepted. This reality means we must accept the wounds to our souls that are caused by evil, and a major part of our acceptance relies on our capacity to grieve for our pain, for the innocence we have lost, and the depths of the effects on our humanity."

Would it be helpful for you to explore them in your journal?

Can you journal about your own capacity to accept and to grieve, and do you realize what your loss of innocence might mean?

As your reflections continue, can you wonder about and explore the ways you may have denied your own grieving process? What effects may you have suffered as a result of this denial?

Can you find some moments in your history where the original word that combines evil and suffering seems appropriate?

What are your personal responses to the following quotation?

"If we cannot face the truth of our losses and our suffering, and find a healing way through them that brings us closer to completing our cycle of transformation, our fear and grief will continue to be increasingly sublimated into anger, aggression, and projecting blame onto other people and groups."

What are your responses to the idea *"... the price of love is grief and being fully human means risking grief for love"*?

Other Thoughts...

CONCLUSION

As I bring these reflections on evil to a close, I want to say that I realize we have followed what may have seemed to be a confusing path between the inner world and the outer world; between the personal and different individuals and groups; between what we think of as our shadows and what we think of as the archetypal nature of evil. The fact is that the nature of what I am talking about is quite confusing. Both shadow and evil have archetypal foundations that are intertwined.

But there is a thread that runs through all of these circumstances around evil that I have been mentioning. That thread is that evil is a call—perhaps, a demand from life for us to develop a more profound sense of self-knowledge and consciousness.

It may help us to remember another well-known quotation from Jung when he passionately says in an interview that, "...the world hangs by a slender thread, and that thread is the consciousness of man...We are the great danger... What if something goes wrong with the psyche?... But we know nothing about it." And it seems that if we are well fed and clothed then we have little urge to learn about ourselves—and that is our greatest mistake of all.

In the few examples I have given, we can see an important truth. Evil as it is symbolized in our shadows is a call for consciousness, for wholeness, and for completing the pattern for the development of our lives that is inherent in our greater Self. And each time we integrate part of our shadow, we reduce the evil in the world. But when we fail to do this, to confront and integrate our shadow, we add to the truth of the statement that the theologian, Reinhold Niebuhr, made in the mid-twentieth century that, "Most evil is not done by evil people, but by good people who don't know what they are doing."

Jung helped us to understand that it is important to become conscious of evil and that we as individuals and as a society cannot learn how to deal with the complexities of evil until we can truly acknowledge evil and confront it as a reality. I believe that the evil we face in the world has the purpose of calling or compelling us out of our childlike state of unconsciousness, our obsession with the "good life," the happy life, the secure life and to force us to engage in the blood, sweat, risks, tears, love, and laughter of real life. And while absolute evil may not be able to be integrated, it can, perhaps, awaken us to our better selves and our need to look for the kind of consciousness that Dr. Jung thought our future depends on.

A NOTE OF THANKS

Whether you received *Confronting Evil* as a gift, borrowed it from a friend, or purchased it yourself, we're glad you read it. We think that Bud Harris is a refreshing, challenging, and inspiring voice and we hope you will share this book and his thoughts with your family and friends. If you would like to learn more about Bud Harris, PhD, and his work, please visit: www.budharris.com and www.facebook.com/BudHarrisPh.D/.

ABOUT THE AUTHOR

Bud Harris, PhD, is a Jungian analyst, writer, and lecturer, who has dedicated his life to help people grow through their challenges and life situations to become "the best versions of themselves."

Originally a corporate businessman, Bud then owned his own business. Though very successful, he began to search for a new version of himself and his life at age thirty-five. He had become dissatisfied with his accomplishments in business and was being challenged by serious illness in his family.

Bud returned to graduate school to study psychotherapy. He earned his PhD in psychology and practiced as a psychotherapist and psychologist for several years. Later, Bud moved to Zurich, Switzerland, where he trained for over five years and graduated from the C. G. Jung Institute to become a Jungian analyst.

Bud is the author of fifteen informing and inspiring books. He writes and teaches with his wife, Jungian analyst Massimilla Harris, PhD, and lectures widely. Bud and Massimilla are practicing Jungian analysts in Asheville, North Carolina. For more information about Bud's practice and work, visit www.budharris.com and www.facebook.com/BudHarrisPh.D/.

Made in the USA
Las Vegas, NV
15 January 2021